That Looks Different!

Stevie Prince

Scientists use electron microscopes to look closely at things. Everyday things often look very different when you look at them through a microscope.

Under a microscope this object looks like bundles of pasta, but it's not.

Can you guess what it is?

It's a T-shirt.

A T-shirt looks different through a microscope. You're seeing the long threads that are woven together to make the fabric.

Under a microscope this object looks like eggs in the dirt, but it's not.

Can you guess what it is?

It's a strawberry.

A strawberry looks different through a microscope. You're seeing the tiny seeds on the outside of the strawberry.

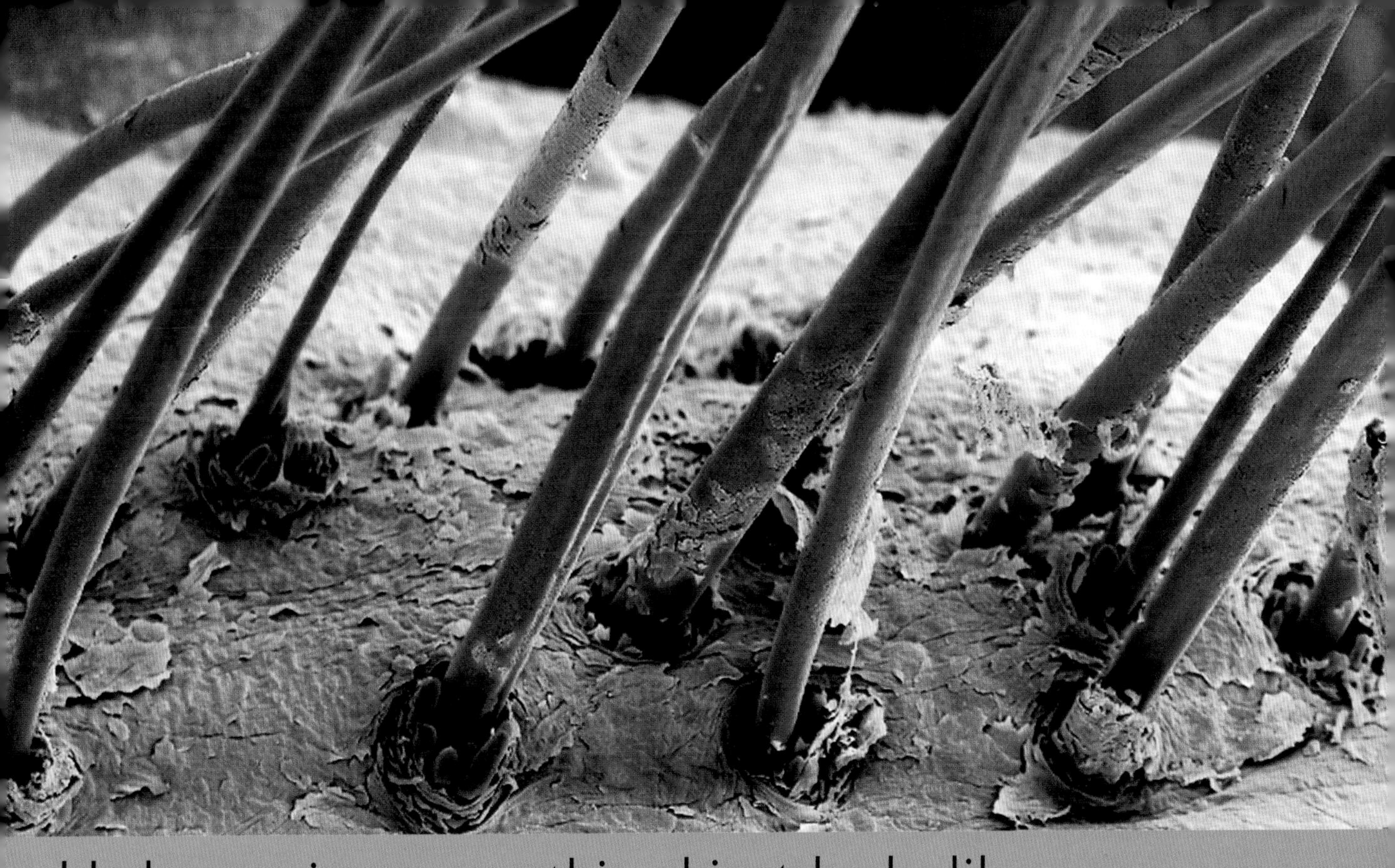

Under a microscope this object looks like grass growing out of the sand, but it's not.

Can you guess what it is?

It's *eyelashes.*

Eyelashes look different through a microscope. You're seeing where the hairs grow out of the skin on an eyelid.

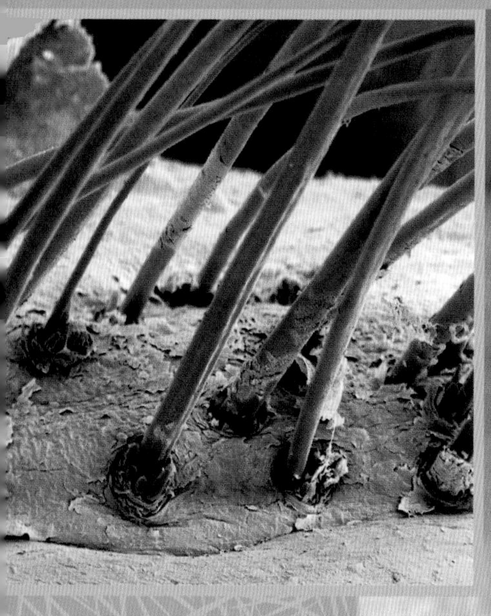

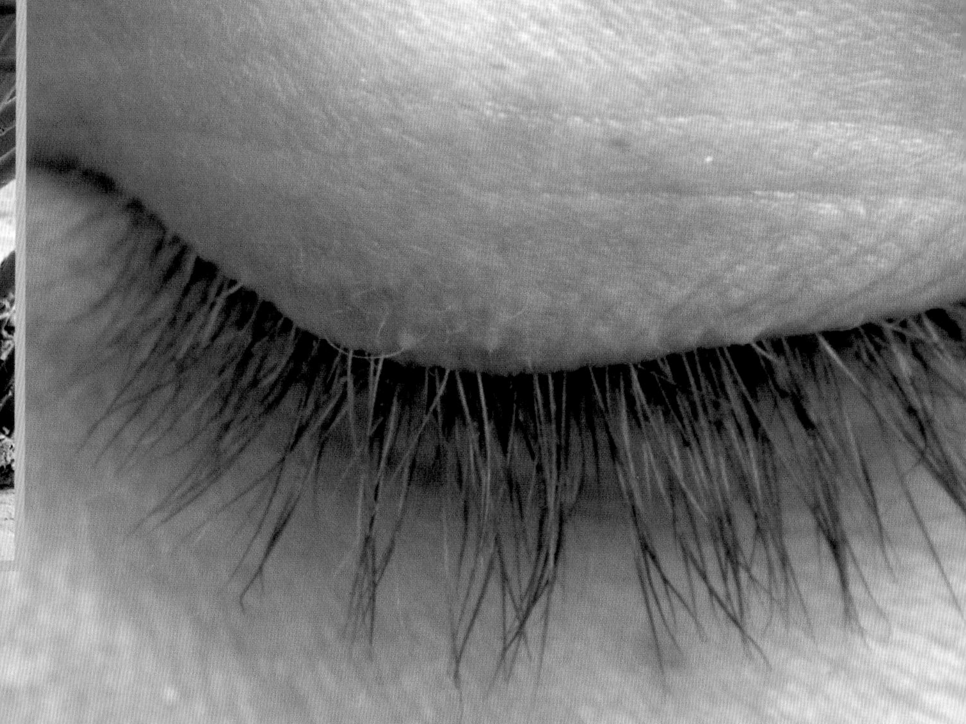

Under a microscope this object looks like tangled wires, but it's not.

Can you guess what it is?

It's a piece of paper.

Paper looks different through a microscope. You're seeing the wood fibers that are pressed together to make paper.

Under a microscope this object looks like an alien, but it's not.

Can you guess what it is?

It's a housefly.

A housefly looks different through a microscope. You're seeing the fly's eyes and antennae up close.

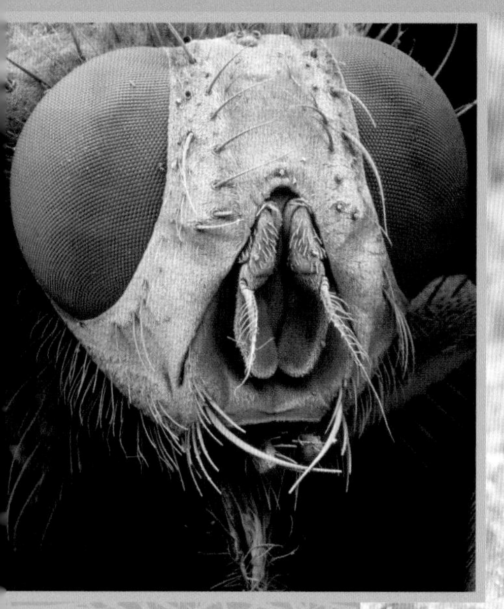